MALCOLM X

A Life From Beginning to End

Copyright © 2018 by Hourly History.

All rights reserved.

Table of Contents

Introduction
A Troubled Childhood
Shining Shoes in Boston
Dealing, Gambling, and Pimping in Harlem
Prison Time
Marriage and Work for the Nation of Islam
Malcolm X Rises to Prominence
Final Years and Assassination
Conclusion

Introduction

Malcolm X was a man whose name was synonymous with fanatical hatred and violence during his lifetime. Fear tended to follow in his footsteps. Gradually, as popular perspectives changed, this same man became remembered in American culture as a champion of human rights. Common sources of knowledge would report that he has been called "one of the greatest and most influential African Americans in history."

Controversies over the true nature and message of this man became less frequent as his prestige grew and schools and libraries were named after him. In 1999, Malcolm X's image was even memorialized on a United States postage stamp. Why did public opinions change so dramatically? How could a man known in his day for bitter, savage hatred become a symbolic hero of human value and human dignity?

The painful, tortuous journeys of Malcolm X's life hold the key to the manifold influences and experiences that shaped this man's brilliant mind. To get a glimpse of the true Malcolm X, you have to walk alongside him. You have to allow yourself to visualize the dark paths through which he passed.

Chapter One

A Troubled Childhood

"We don't have time for the white man ... We are working on our own people."

—Malcolm X

As members of the Universal Negro Improvement Association, Earl and Louise Little passed on a tremendous fervor for their cause to their seven children. The objective of the Littles was not advancement of humanity as a whole; they did not work toward broad religious, patriotic, or altruistic goals. The focus of the Littles was strictly narrowed to the betterment of conditions for African Americans at a time when racism ran rampant in the United States.

Reverend Earl Little was a Baptist preacher in Omaha, Nebraska, who encouraged others to accept the "Back to Africa" philosophies of Marcus Garvey, rejecting interracial marriage and advocating complete separation of the races. His wife, Louise, was pregnant with their fourth child when Ku Klux Klan members delivered threats of violence to the Little family. That child was born on May 19, 1925, as Malcolm Little.

Fearing for their safety, the family soon moved to Milwaukee, Wisconsin and then on to Lansing, Michigan.

Reverend Little's ambition was to find a lifestyle in which he could be completely independent of people who did not share his skin color. However, in Lansing the Littles received threats from the black community who did not appreciate the reverend's purist ideals. They were also harassed by a white supremacist group called the Black Legion.

In 1929, just after Malcolm's younger sister was born, the family's house was set on fire. The family barely escaped before the house collapsed. Later, Malcolm would feel that policemen and firemen had watched with complete indifference. Finally, Reverend Little built a small house for his family in the countryside. Their home was not free from strife; Earl often squabbled with his wife, sometimes physically abusing her, and treated his children harshly.

Malcolm did not respect his father's preaching or the teachings of Christianity, but he did have a great fascination for the principles of Marcus Garvey. The young boy attended meetings in individual homes of the Universal Negro Improvement Association along with his father. He listened to doctrines of black race superiority, stared in awe at flamboyant photographs of Garvey in parade, and felt inspired by the earnestness of the Association members.

Malcolm experienced the effects of racial prejudices in his own home, where he believed that his parents treated him differently because his skin was a slightly lighter shade than that of his siblings. And so, the little boy developed a system of manipulating his parents and others through making a great fuss until he was given what he wanted. He had his own little garden in which he found a sense of peace and in which he especially loved to work to grow peas for the family. At five years old, he began attending the Pleasant Grove School.

In 1931, following a typical argument, Louise had a strong presentiment of coming tragedy for her husband. Later that night, policemen arrived to take her to the hospital, where Reverend Earl Little lay mutilated after being run over by a streetcar. Six-year-old Malcolm received the news of his father's death the next morning. Although Earl's death was officially ruled as an accident, many family friends wondered if he had been deliberately murdered by the Black Legion, the same terrorist organization Earl had claimed burned down their house a couple of years before. Understandably, Malcolm's mother was hysterical.

The life insurance company came up with a different story, however, and claimed that Reverend Little had committed suicide, thus negating their responsibility to pay out his life insurance policy. The oldest of the Little children quit his education to get a job to support the family. Disturbed by these recent events, Malcolm got into fistfights at school and struggled to find his place at home.

Louise was able to get odd jobs in town. Malcolm felt that these jobs only lasted until her identity as a black woman was discovered—she was extremely light-skinned since her father was a white man. The Great Depression was beginning, and the Little family was battling to survive. Finally, the state welfare agency became involved.

Caseworkers intruded on the Little home, asking questions and inspecting the house. In spite of Mrs. Little's disinclination to give the state control over her family, she was forced to accept the meager welfare checks and other forms of public charity that were offered to them.

By 1934, the Littles were sustaining themselves by eating day-old bread from the bakery and boiled dandelion greens from their yard. Finding themselves still dizzy with hunger, the boys shot rabbits and cut off bullfrog's legs to sell to kindly neighbors. Malcolm also began begging meals from friends. He stole produce from stores in town or from farmer's fields. At less than ten years old, Malcolm was already earning a bad reputation for himself.

Within a couple of years, Louise began dating a man who reminded Malcolm a bit of his father. When the man ultimately left her, Malcolm's mother disintegrated emotionally. The burden of trying to care for her family alone was too much for her, and the failed relationship had left her pregnant, with yet another mouth to feed. State welfare workers intervened and began to distribute the Little children among neighbors and foster homes.

At 12 years of age, Malcolm went to live with the Gohannes, a strongly religious elderly couple that he already knew and liked. Along with the Gohannes's nephew, who lived with them, Malcolm now attended the Lansing West Junior High School, but he did not make new friends easily. Life became more stable, however. Malcolm went fishing and hunting for rabbits with his new family and their friends. He was also able to visit his mother frequently until her deteriorating condition made it necessary for her to be consigned to the psychiatric hospital at Kalamazoo, over 70 miles away from Lansing. Louise would stay at the hospital for the next 24 years.

Wanting to follow his older brother's lead and gain distinction for himself in high school boxing, Malcolm signed up in 1937 and tried a couple of fights. In spite of the initial support of his family and friends and a lot of effort in the gym, Malcolm lost both bouts. He was humiliated. Since his opponent was a white boy, Malcolm felt that he had irreparably lost face among the black community. Shortly afterward, Malcolm deliberately went into his school classroom still wearing his hat, which was against the rules. When the teacher disciplined him, Malcolm responded by covertly putting a tack on the instructor's chair. As a result, Malcolm was expelled from school.

At 13 years of age, Malcolm Little was sent by the state to a detention home in Mason, Michigan. His foster family wept with grief when Malcolm was taken from their home. At the detention home, Malcolm was treated kindly and given his own room for the first time in his life. Nonetheless, the white people around him habitually used offensive terms to refer to people of his skin color. They would talk about Malcolm and other black people in ways that were highly insensitive, seemingly unaware or unconcerned about Malcolm's listening ears. Although Malcolm was now respectful and industrious, he became increasingly irritated by the condescension showed toward him by white people.

In the evenings, Malcolm was permitted to loiter about the streets, bars, and restaurants of Lansing on his own. Eventually he was enrolled in the seventh grade of the Mason Junior High School, a predominantly white school. Malcolm's improved attitude and natural intelligence made him popular in his classes with both students and teachers.

Soon Malcolm's friends at the detention home helped him to get a job at a restaurant so that he would have spending money of his own. He was on the school basketball team, which he enjoyed. His grades were among the best in his class. He was even elected class president. Life was good.

All too frequently, however, ugly evidence of racial prejudice simply could not be ignored. Malcolm's white school teachers casually made cruel derogatory jokes about African Americans in class. At dances, Malcolm could not mingle with the white girls. No matter how hard he tried to fit in, he was faced with remarks and incidents that convinced him that he was not truly considered an equal by his white friends.

In 1940, at 15 years of age, Malcolm traveled to Boston to visit his older half-sister Ella, one of three of his father's children by a previous marriage. "From my seat in—you guessed it—the back of the bus, I gawked out of the window at white man's America rolling past," Malcolm later remembered. When he arrived in Roxbury, Boston, however, Malcolm was introduced to a vibrant black community such as he had never seen or even dreamed of before.

Back in Lansing after summer vacation had come to an end, Malcolm experienced a rising discontent as he remembered the life he had experienced in the city of Boston. The final straw came when Malcolm's English teacher, in spite of his excellent grades, belittled his ambition to become a lawyer, telling him that he should choose a career considered more realistic for someone of his race, perhaps in carpentry.

Sensing Malcolm's restlessness, his friends at the detention home sent him to live with another foster family, hoping to give him some happiness. Angry inside over the racial prejudices he had faced, Malcolm would not discuss his feelings with anyone. Instead, he wrote a letter to his half-sister Ella simply asking to come to Boston to live with her. Ella managed to get custody of Malcolm reassigned to the state of Massachusetts. "All praise is due to Allah that I went to Boston when I did," Malcolm would later write. "If I hadn't, I'd probably still be a brainwashed black Christian."

Chapter Two

Shining Shoes in Boston

"Usually the black racist has been produced by the white racist. . . . If we react to white racism with a violent reaction, to me that's not black racism. If you come to put a rope around my neck and I hang you for it, to me that's not racism. Yours is racism, but my reaction has nothing to do with racism."

—Malcolm X

At first, Malcolm was impressed with the sophisticated, homeowning black community who lived in Roxbury, Boston. Later, he came to realize that these people had prejudices of their own, often looking down on those of their race who were less fortunate than themselves. Malcolm came to despise these successful African American citizens and their somewhat pretentious exhibitions of prosperity, considering them spineless imitators of white culture.

Instead, Malcolm was drawn to the ghettos of Roxbury. There he made a friend who got him a job as a shoeshiner at the Roseland State Ballroom. Malcolm quickly learned that the way to make money as a shoeshiner involved providing liquor, marijuana, and prostitutes to his customers at the ballroom. Soon

Malcolm was involved himself in drinking, smoking marijuana, and gambling. He also submitted to a homemade treatment for straightening his hair. "This was my first really big step toward self-degradation: when I endured all of that pain, literally burning my flesh to have it look like a white man's hair," he later remembered with shame. "If [black people] gave the brains in their heads just half as much attention as they do their hair, they would be a thousand times better off."

When he learned to dance, Malcolm gave up his job polishing shoes. He would attend dances at the Roseland Ballroom himself now and work as a soda fountain clerk at the Townsend Drug Store a couple blocks from Ella's house. In the meanwhile, Malcolm's aversion to the homeowning black community on "the Hill" grew. He scorned their ostentatious habit of giving their menial jobs elaborate titles. He despised their affected accents, which were not like the dialect that he felt was the true speech of African Americans. Malcolm assumed that by wishing to integrate with the culture of other Americans instead of confining themselves to a black subculture, the Hill people were not being true to their nature.

Contradictorily, Malcolm himself deliberately neglected his budding relationship with an intelligent, high-caliber young African American girl simply in order to cultivate the social status of having a white girlfriend. Having somewhat alienated himself from his half-sister Ella by his behavior, he moved into a friend's apartment and got a job as a busboy at the Parker House restaurant.

When the Japanese bombed Pearl Harbor in 1941, 16-year-old Malcolm lied about his age in order get a job as a dishwasher for the Yankee Clipper railway. He made his first visits to Washington, D.C. during overnight layovers of the train. There he was disturbed to discover two widely varying black communities—one living in horrifyingly abject poverty while the other, although educated and much more prosperous, was nonetheless limited to unskilled jobs.

Next the railway took Malcolm to Harlem in New York City. The result was similar to that of his first visit to Boston a couple of years before; he became restless with the allure of the larger city and the fascination of the electrifying black community of Harlem. Malcolm was no longer content in Roxbury.

Chapter Three

Dealing, Gambling, and Pimping in Harlem

"I believe in treating people right, but I'm not going to waste my time trying to treat somebody right who doesn't return the treatment."

—Malcolm X

It wasn't long before Malcolm was fired from his job on the railway for using profanity toward customers and exhibiting generally uncontrolled behavior. He decided to pay a visit back home to Lansing. At over six feet tall, wearing the infamous billowing zoot suit popular in the ghettos and boiling over with ghetto slang, Malcolm caused a sensation among his siblings and friends—though not always an unreservedly pleasant one.

The visit over, Malcolm naturally headed for New York City, where he found another railway job, this time on the Seaboard Line. The new job did not last very long, either. After being fired from his second railway job in 1942, 17-year-old Malcolm was offered a position as a waiter in Small's Paradise, a bar in Harlem. As a waiter, Malcolm was handsome, efficient, and agreeable enough to attract the attention of the bartenders and regular customers. These wealthy African Americans began to take Malcolm under their wings and offer him an interesting sort of education—the history and culture of Harlem, the intricacies of the pervading gambling scene, and the secrets of their particular hustles, the carefully developed scams and other illegal activities that kept them rich.

Malcolm learned to identify plainclothes authorities and recognize dangerous gang members. He made friends with a pimp named Sammy and boarded in an apartment filled with prostitutes. There his education was further expanded, and his opinions about women were formed. "All women, by their nature, are fragile and weak," he would later state. "They are attracted to the male in whom they see strength."

Nicknamed "Detroit Red" because of the red-tinted hair he had inherited from his white grandfather, Malcolm was certainly learning his way around town when he was caught proffering prostitutes to customers. He was fired from the bar to protect its status, but Sammy gave him tips toward getting started as a fulltime drug dealer.

Malcolm was staggered at how quickly he could make significant amounts of cash by supplying the well-known musicians of Harlem with marijuana. He began carrying a pistol and working out stratagems for evading the police. When his activities became so notorious that the Harlem narcotics squad had him particularly marked for investigation, he moved his area of operations to lower Harlem. There, among the poorest in the ghettos, it was much harder to make money peddling drugs. Further advice from Sammy made Malcolm realize that he could use the railway ID card still in his possession to travel for free, selling marijuana to Harlem bands on the road.

In 1943, Malcolm received his draft notice from the United States government, which was involved in World War II. Malcolm dressed as crazily as possible and faked near insanity when he came before the draft board. He pretended wild and extraordinary enthusiasm for entering the war, culminated by his whispering to the psychological evaluator that he ultimately hoped to steal guns with which to murder white men. Unsurprisingly, Malcolm was excused from the draft.

When he flashed his pistol during a gambling argument in the railway locker room, Malcolm's days of riding the train for free were over. He turned to robbery and gambling, using cocaine to bolster himself for dangerous stickups.

When Malcolm's younger brother Reginald arrived in Harlem to live with him, Malcolm showed him around town and instructed him in how to earn a legal, though dishonest, living by pretending to sell stolen goods. Reginald actually had the license necessary to market the cheap trinkets that he had purchased and resold as more valuable items.

After racial riots broke out in Harlem, it became much more difficult for the brothers to survive. Most of the black community had formerly existed on the money brought into Harlem by white customers. Now that fear had driven the white nightlife away, hunger and need came in their place. African Americans who had lived "by their wits" were suddenly forced to look for jobs. Malcolm attempted ever riskier robberies.

One burglary nearly ended in the death of Sammy, Malcolm's criminal partner. Afterward, Malcolm struck one of the pimp's beautiful prostitutes, who was angry at him because of the gunshot injury Sammy had incurred. Sammy quickly pulled a gun on Malcolm, and the prostitute had to help Malcolm to escape. Although the two men were later reconciled, Malcolm had lost the only fully trusting relationship he had. He began to turn more completely to his younger brother Reginald for companionship, instructing him to work for a short time for the railway so that he could acquire an ID card that would later permit him to travel for free, just as Malcolm had done earlier.

In the meanwhile, Malcolm joined a gambling racket and learned even more about political corruption and the criminal world. "Crime existed only to the degree that the law cooperated with it," he would later write. "In the country's entire social, political, and economic structure, the criminal, the law, and the politicians were actually inseparable partners."

Malcolm also became more deeply involved in an even darker side of Harlem—the sex market. He was paid for directing wealthy, prominent white men, usually middle-aged or older, to certain African American prostitutes who would agree to accommodate especially perverted sexual appetites. Although he himself was willingly participating in the business to make a few extra dollars, the depravities that Malcolm witnessed during this time effectively destroyed any remnants of respect that he might have felt for white people. It is also said that Malcolm himself occasionally sold sexual services to men for money.

Eventually Malcolm's health began to deteriorate. Using opium as well as marijuana, he moved through a fog. He turned to transporting illegal liquor to support himself until the operation was wrecked by the State Liquor Authority. When a gambling argument left Malcolm's life threatened by one of the toughest members of the black community, he boosted his courage with opium, Benzedrine tablets, marijuana, and cocaine simultaneously. So high that he seemed to be moving through a dream world, Malcolm got into a fistfight with a young man in a bar. He was able to discard his gun only moments before the police closed in to investigate, thus narrowly evading arrest.

Knowing that he was being backed into an inescapable corner, Malcolm readily agreed to leave Harlem when an old friend from Boston responded to Sammy's telephone call for help and arrived to rescue him.

Chapter Four

Prison Time

"You trust them (white Americans), and I don't. You studied what he wanted you to learn about him in schools. I studied him in the streets and in prison, where you see the truth."

—Malcolm X

"I believed that a man should do anything that he was slick enough, or bad and bold enough, to do and that a woman was nothing but another commodity," Malcolm later wrote about this period of his life. "Every word I spoke was hip or profane. I would bet that my working vocabulary wasn't two hundred words. I lived and thought like a predatory animal."

At last in safety with his friend in Boston, Malcolm slept, smoked marijuana, listened to music, and slept some more, as his exhausted body tried to recover from the drug abuse and stress it had suffered. After a couple of weeks, Malcolm began to look up old friends and become involved in the gambling scene in Boston, trying to support his drug addictions. Soon Malcolm had organized a professional burglary ring involving himself, his friend, another young black man, Malcolm's longtime white girlfriend, and her younger sister. The girls would scope out potential scenes for robbery, communicate their findings, and the thefts would be successfully carried out by the men during the night. The money rolled in, and Malcolm drowned any anxieties with cocaine and marijuana.

The inevitable denouement came when Malcolm took a stolen watch to a jewelry shop for repairs. Faced by the police, Malcolm gave up his gun and accepted arrest. As he was questioned about his activities, Malcolm was convinced that these white men were much angrier over his involvement with white girls than they were over his numerous crimes.

In February of 1946, at 20 years of age, Malcolm Little was sentenced to eight to ten years in jail. In Massachusetts' Charlestown State Prison, Malcolm would have to endure drug withdrawal in a cell so small that he could touch both walls from his cot, tormented by the pervading filthiness and the inescapable smells from the bucket that served as a toilet. Fiercely bitter, often swearing savagely at friend and foe alike, Malcolm learned to get high using nutmeg bribed from the kitchen prison. When he was given money, he bought marijuana, Nembutal, and Benzedrine tablets from the guards. Even his cellmates began to nickname him "Satan" for his defiant behavior and often-voiced hatred for Christianity.

An intelligent and respected inmate of the prison suggested to Malcolm that he should read the books from the prison library and also take advantage of the correspondence courses offered to prisoners. Malcolm had earned some of the top grades in his school when he graduated from eighth grade. Now he began to work to review what he had learned and improve his education, even studying Latin.

Malcolm was transferred to the Concord Prison in 1947. There he received letters from two of his brothers who had converted to an American version of the Muslim religion, which they believed to be the natural religion for black-skinned people. Vaguely convinced that their advice would help him to escape from prison, Malcolm was persuaded to quit eating pork and smoking cigarettes.

In 1948, Malcolm was relocated to the Prison Colony in Norfolk, Massachusetts, through the efforts of his half-sister Ella. The conditions in this prison were much better, granting more space, conveniences, and fresh air to the inmates. The schooling opportunities offered to prisoners were provided by instructors from high-quality institutions such as Harvard. The library was immense. Malcolm took advantage of it all. In Norfolk, Malcolm received a visit from his younger brother Reginald. During the visit, Reginald stated to Malcolm that Allah (the Arabic term for "god") had visited America and knows everything. He also averred that Satan rules people through the secret fraternity of the Masons.

Reginald went on to contend that Muslims had managed to specifically identify Satan. "The white man is the devil," Reginald explained, insisting that every white person is consciously aware of being a reigning force of evil, especially if they belong to the Masons. Every single member of the white race is deliberately involved in defrauding and exploiting the superior black race worldwide, Reginald maintained. Embittered by the egregious racial prejudices he had endured and the heinous evil he had witnessed in the dregs of society, Malcolm was not slow to embrace these ideas for himself. "The white man is the devil," became Malcolm Little's own motto.

Soon Malcolm was receiving no end of letters from his siblings and their families, who had converted to this version of Islam. The letters described an African American from Georgia called Elijah Muhammad, whom the family had met. Elijah claimed that he had met god, who he believed to be a man named Wallace Fard, in Detroit. Malcolm was strongly advised to begin practicing the religious restrictions of Islam, avoiding drugs and alcohol as well as pork and cigarettes.

Malcolm came to believe that all written history had been falsified by white people. He was taught that from the beginning black people had ruled the whole earth in wisdom and prosperity until devilish white people emerged from caves and began their wicked exploitation of the superior race. Reflecting on America's shameful history of slavery and racial prejudice, Malcolm found these theories easy to accept. He also readily adopted the idea that Christianity was invented merely as a tool to convince black people to passively accept the diabolical injustices forced upon them by white society.

Seeing that Malcolm believed the doctrines perpetrated by Wallace Fard, his siblings taught him more. Black people, they explained, had built the first civilizations and founded the city of Mecca at the very beginning of the world. This early civilization included 24 scientists, one of whom had the ability to create a particularly strong tribe named the Shabazz, from whom African Americans would later descend.

About 6,600 years ago, however, an incredibly intelligent man named Yakub was born. Yakub became a scientist who spread dissatisfaction among the people. He gained a following of 59,999 followers whom Allah exiled with him to the island of Patmos. Angry over his exile, Yakub slowly used his scientific knowledge to breed a devil race—the white people. It took 600 years of careful breeding before the white race fully emerged and populated the island of Patmos, long after Yakub's death of old age. They eventually found their way off the island and began spreading dissension among the peaceful, prosperous civilization of the black people in Mecca.

At last the black people realized the trouble that the white race was causing. They clothed them with small aprons, put them in chains, and exiled them, this time to the caves of Europe. Another 2,000 years passed in which the white people lived as savages in the caves. Finally, Allah granted the white race a leader named Moses. The first of the white people to be liberated from the caves by Moses were called Jews. Their history is symbolically represented in the Bible. Thus, the white people crept from their caves, and during the subsequent centuries they persecuted and exploited the superior black race from whom they had been nefariously derived.

Malcolm believed that every single white person was a self-aware devil who purposely participated in the abominable practice of enslaving black people for his own advantages.

Wallace Fard, honored as the mightiest god by his African American followers, claimed to be half black and half white, according to Malcolm's siblings. In 1931, Fard had met Elijah Muhammad and instructed him to establish a new religion called the Nation of Islam (NOI). This religion was to lead the black people to overthrow all white rule and regain domination of the world.

Although he wholeheartedly accepted the doctrines of the Nation of Islam and even wrote daily letters to Elijah Muhammad, Malcolm found it difficult to humble himself to actually pray to Allah. He also tried to express his newfound faith to his old friends through letters, but he received no answers.

Meanwhile, Malcolm continued his education. He learned vocabulary and practiced his penmanship at the same time by laboriously copying every page of an entire dictionary. Malcolm no longer noticed the passing days or felt imprisoned as the world of books and knowledge opened before him through the prison library, educational classes, and debate clubs. Long after lights were supposed to be out, Malcolm read by the glow of light seeping into his cell from the prison hallway.

Malcolm learned about the prestigious history of nonwhite peoples, something that had not been taught in the schools of his childhood. He studied Gregor Mendel's famous researches in genetics and learned that it is scientifically true that the white gene is recessive and that humanity's original ancestors could not have been completely white-skinned. Even the atrocities of slavery in America were first truly realized by Malcolm through books from the prison library. Horrified and enraged at the inhuman treatment of black slaves by their white kidnappers, Malcolm was drawn to the history of violent reformers such as John Brown and Nat Turner, who formed bands of slaves to kill white supporters of slavery.

History books taught Malcolm about the imperialism practiced by white races in countries such as England, which ruthlessly exploited entire nations of darker-skinned people through such machinations as the East India Company. It paraded before him all of the dirty laundry of the Christian religion—how so-called Christian people felt justified in destroying and exploiting people whom they labeled as "pagans," and how the peaceable, loving teachings of Jesus were often ignored by those who claimed to be his followers.

With the evidence of egregious human sinfulness throughout history thus exposed to his mind, Malcolm forgot his own recent perpetration of wicked, exploitive practices—or more accurately, Malcolm chose to blame his personal behavior on others. Though he described himself as having "prey[ed] upon other human beings like a hawk or a vulture," Malcolm became more and more convinced that "history proves that the white man is a devil," responsible for all the world's ills, including any crimes committed by a black person.

"You will never catch me with a free fifteen minutes in which I'm not studying something I feel might be able to help the black man," Malcolm would later write. Books had opened a world before Malcolm that he had never dreamed existed. As he learned about the great achievements of dark-skinned civilizations, the truth slowly suffused his mind; all of his life, the racial prejudices of America had pervaded his environment so completely that he had subconsciously considered his own race to be inferior. Now Malcolm was elated by the realization that dark-skinned people were in no way less valuable than people with light skin.

As Malcolm came to respect his African American heritage, however, he also increasingly despised the white heritage that came to him from his unknown grandfather. "I learned to hate every drop of that white rapist's blood that is in me," he declaimed.

The first snag in his spiritual journey appeared when Malcolm's younger brother Reginald was suspended from the new religious group for an illicit sexual relationship with the secretary of the Nation of Islam's New York temple. Upset and confused, Malcolm wrote a letter to Elijah Muhammad and prayed fervently to Allah, begging for mercy for his brother. That night, Malcolm visualized Wallace Fard, the man acclaimed as the omniscient god of the Nation of Islam. Soon, he received a letter from Elijah that encouraged him to repudiate the wrong choices of his brother and strengthen his submission to the Nation of Islam. Malcolm agreed, feeling that his identity as a Muslim was stronger than his family ties. Eventually, facing the rejection of his entire family, Malcolm's younger brother would deteriorate physically and then become deranged, claiming to be greater than Allah.

Reginald was ultimately institutionalized, just as his mother had been long ago.

Malcolm was transferred back to the Charlestown Prison for his last year of incarceration. He would have to begin wearing glasses since his eyesight was permanently damaged from hours of late-night reading by the dim light from the hallway of the Concord Prison. The Massachusetts State Parole Board granted Malcolm Little's release from prison on parole in 1952. He would be under the custody of his oldest brother Wilfred in the ghetto of Detroit.

Chapter Five

Marriage and Work for the Nation of Islam

"While a man must at all times respect his woman, at the same time he needs to understand that he must control her if he expects to get her respect."

—Malcolm X

In the furniture store that Wilfred managed in Detroit, Malcolm watched as African Americans foolishly purchased low-quality home furnishings on credit for exorbitantly high interest rates. Every experience seemed to cement his growing hatred for the white race and his expanding respect for the Nation of Islam. Malcolm would live with Wilfred's family in his home, where the ritual cleansings, greetings, prayers, and dietary restrictions of the Muslim world were scrupulously observed. To Malcolm, whose life had known nothing but conflict for so many years, it seemed like a slice of heaven.

Three times a week, the family attended the Detroit Temple Number One, originally founded by Wallace Fard. Malcolm was overwhelmed by the quiet, conservative, respectful lifestyles of his new friends. He was also eager to recruit more believers to the small congregation. Wilfred advised him to wait until he had met the man known as Elijah Muhammad for himself.

On August 31, 1952, Malcolm watched and listened in awe as the man from Georgia who called himself the Messenger of Allah paraded ceremoniously into Temple Number Two in Chicago. After a speech detailing his personal sufferings for the cause and his hopes for worldwide dominance of the black race, Elijah suddenly asked Malcolm Little to stand. In grand terms, Elijah praised and encouraged Malcolm's faithful adherence to the newly founded religion of the Nation of Islam.

After the service, Elijah invited the Little family to a meal in his sumptuous home in Chicago. There, Malcolm received advice from the leader himself on invigorating the temple in Detroit; he should begin by recruiting young people. Malcolm entered into the work with enthusiasm. First, he changed his last name, which had been bestowed upon his family by a slave owner in the past. Malcolm Little became Malcolm X, according to the traditions of the Nation of Islam.

Within a few months, Elijah Muhammad arrived to personally commend Malcolm and the rest of Temple One for increasing their membership to three times the number that had belonged to the group when Malcolm first attended.

By 1953, Malcolm was established enough in his new life to find his own home and a janitor's job at the Gar Wood vehicle factory in Detroit. He was appointed as assistant minister at the temple and spoke with fierce passion of his hatred of the white race and the wrongs they had inflicted on African Americans.

It wasn't long before Malcolm was again drafted for service in the military. First, Malcolm lied about not realizing that he should have registered for the draft. Then he registered as a Muslim conscientious objector. Once again, he was excused. Malcolm now found a job at a Ford Motor Company and spent much of his free time with Elijah Muhammad and his family, absorbing the teachings of the Nation of Islam.

Soon Malcolm decided that he should dedicate his time even more exclusively to the new religion. He quit his job and began receiving training in its occult lore in order to become a minister. Elijah taught him in his own home in Chicago and permitted him to travel with him to Boston as well, where Malcolm spoke to new recruits, stirring up anger against white people by recounting the past barbarities of the slave trade. Soon a new temple could be opened in Boston through Malcolm's dramatic eloquence and fiery passion. By May of 1954, less than three months later, he had organized a temple in Philadelphia as well. Now he would be sent to New York City.

At first, Malcolm struggled to find converts in Harlem. The people of the ghetto were already so choked with bitterness that one more voice spewing a doctrine of anger and hatred did not garner much attention. Malcolm and his small congregation tried passing out tracts on street corners and at the edges of crowds who had gathered to hear other speakers. They sought the attention of people leaving their churches on Sunday mornings, trying to convince them that Christianity was deliberately invented by the white race in order to demean and enslave darker-skinned people.

Malcolm blamed his inability to immediately interest the people of Harlem in the Nation of Islam on its strict rules, which were actively enforced by a sort of Muslim police titled the Fruit of Islam (FOI). These religious leaders required clean, moral living of their people, which eliminated behaviors such as illicit sex, substance abuse, lying, stealing, gambling, and law-breaking. However, entertainments such as dancing, dating, watching movies, enjoying sports, or even taking a vacation were also prohibited. In addition to performing a round of daily rituals and attending services at the temple, members of the Nation of Islam were expected to observe strict dietary laws. Even the amount of sleep enjoyed each night was to be regulated according to religious law.

But Malcolm was untiring in his efforts to bring new converts to his beloved religion. He continued speaking in Philadelphia. He established a new temple in Springfield, Massachusetts, and another in Hartford, Connecticut. In 1955, he was sent to open a temple in Atlanta, Georgia. By 1956, Malcolm needed a car to enable him to carry on his work for the Nation of Islam, so the religious group supplied him with one.

In spite of the Muslim prohibition against dating and his own deep mistrust of women, Malcolm asked a female convert from the New York temple to go with him on an outing to the Museum of Natural History, ostensibly to increase her knowledge of points in the Nation of Islam doctrine. Betty was an attractive and intelligent woman currently attending a college of nursing.

After receiving Elijah's approval, Malcolm abruptly called Betty on the telephone and asked her to marry him in 1958, arranging to pick her up at her foster parents' home and take her immediately to be married by a Justice of the Peace. Determined to avoid all romance or indulgence toward the bride, Malcolm refused to kiss Betty after the ceremony.

Chapter Six

Malcolm X Rises to Prominence

"We cannot think of uniting with others, until after we have first united among ourselves. We cannot think of being acceptable to others until we have first proven acceptable to ourselves."

—Malcolm X

Malcolm and Betty lived together in Queens in New York City. Like thousands of other members of the Nation of Islam, they would be known as the X family. Malcolm had also taken on the name of Malcolm Shabazz (or Malik el-Shabazz) after the original name of the African American people—Tribe of Shabazz—according to the Nation of Islam myths.

The Nation of Islam began receiving media attention after April 26, 1957, when a member refused to leave the scene of a street fight. He was viciously beaten with nightsticks by the police. Malcolm and a mob of 50 Muslim men gathered outside the police station in protest, joined by hundreds of other angry African Americans. Malcolm informed the police that the men would not be leaving until they were assured that their brother would receive proper care. After an ambulance had transported the man (who had suffered brain contusions and subdural hemorrhaging) to the hospital, Malcolm signaled for the Nation of Islam protesters to disband, and the crowd, who had grown to about 4,000 people, all dispersed peacefully.

Malcolm's emotions seethed with pity for the victim, animosity toward the bloodthirsty policemen, pride in the success of the Nation of Islam's protest, and great hope that the event would lead to further growth for the new religion.

Malcolm and Betty's oldest daughter was born a few months later, on November 16, 1958. She was named Attallah, after Attila the Hun, the dark-skinned barbarian who brutally conquered the white-skinned Romans in ancient times.

Malcolm's hopes for publicity were realized in 1959 when Nation of Islam temples, ministers, and congregations were filmed for a documentary on the Mike Wallace Show. The production, titled *The Hate That Hate Produced*, shocked and frightened people of all shades of color as it clearly revealed the hostility of the Nation of Islam's beliefs. Malcolm was hugely irritated at the public's reaction. He felt that his virulent hatred of all white people was justified in light of the horrific past abuses of slavery and the injustices still caused by racial prejudice.

Bombarded by telephone calls, newspaper articles, and interviews, Malcolm spit his malice for white-skinned people and his dedication to complete segregation and an eventual black supremacy right back into the faces of an accusing society. When asked if he knew of any single white man who was a good person and not a devil, Malcolm would list two—Hitler and Stalin, for their murder of masses of white-skinned people.

However, Malcolm's bitterest attacks were often directed toward African Americans who were appalled at his hate-filled teachings. Malcolm accused them of being mere puppets of white leaders, calling them "trained black parrots" and refusing to accredit them with any personal integrity or dignity. In television and radio interviews, Malcolm simply outshouted his debate opponents, ridiculing the mere idea of racial integration, denouncing Christianity's teachings of peace, and reiterating his belief that all white people were abusive devils who could never be trusted.

The furor quickly attracted crowds of curious African Americans to the Nation of Islam meetings. Elijah Muhammad now addressed more than 10,000 people in gatherings to which white people were originally not admitted. These religious services were widely publicized by reporters as public uneasiness over the dangerous cult increased. At these gatherings, Malcolm exercised his American rights of assembly and free speech, protected by the Constitution and the array of policemen who were necessary to guard the event, as he proclaimed that "Our enemy is the white man! You are living in pure hell on this earth, while he lives in pure heaven right on this same earth! That devil is our enemy!"

Malcolm frequently ridiculed advocates of nonviolence during the meetings and perpetrated the idea that black people could never feel at home in the land of America, though notably he did not seek to relocate with his own family to another country. Malcolm also seemed to resent being called racist, anti-white, or a teacher of hate even though hatred of the white race had always been the center of his message.

No one could deny, however, that the Nation of Islam was doing great good for many African Americans whose lives had been devastated by the vices of the ghettos. The religion's high moral standards, strict Fruit of Islam conduct police, and highly effective social reform programs helped many to escape their drug, alcohol, and tobacco addictions and immoral lifestyles. The basis of much of the good that was accomplished for African Americans came from the vehement reassurance that they were truly valuable human beings. The constant burden of having endured racial prejudices from childhood, coupled with the shame of their own debased lifestyles, had left many African Americans demoralized. When they were consistently encouraged, instructed, and helped by others who had escaped the corruption of the ghettos and who treated them with respect and confidence, they were inspirited to make changes in their own lives as well.

Nonetheless, in spite of his frequently expressed teachings that the black community must stand on its own without any dependence on any white person, Malcolm was incongruously resentful when the government did not subsidize the Nation of Islam's drug rehabilitation programs.

In his personal life, Malcolm welcomed a second daughter to his home in December of 1960. This child was named Qubilah after Kublai Khan, an Asian imperialist. Two more daughters and then twin sisters would follow, making a total of six little girls in the family. Malcolm himself was seldom at home with his family, however, always traveling on behalf of the Nation of Islam.

By 1961, the Nation of Islam had expanded to the point that they could afford the construction of a beautiful $20 million Islamic Center in Chicago. The religious organization had its own newspaper and radio stations. Nation of Islam elementary schools had even been built in Chicago and Detroit.

Meanwhile, Elijah Muhammad, suffering from ill health, began to turn many of the responsibilities of the Nation of Islam over to Malcolm. Perhaps feeling the weight of his new authority, Malcolm subtly began to change his message. No longer did he publicly accuse every single white person of being a literal devil who deliberately exploited darker-skinned people. Instead, Malcolm redefined his terms to indicate that "we are speaking of the collective white man's historical record."

But one thing that didn't change was Malcolm's contempt for educated African American leaders who advocated racial integration. He maintained that the universal guilt of the white race made them afraid "that God wrathfully is going to destroy this civilization" and that white men would never willingly tolerate a black man marrying a white woman.

Regardless of his undying animosity toward white America, Malcolm was often a powerful inspiration to the African American community. Under his influence, dark-skinned people began to realize and accept the natural beauty of their own bodies and celebrate their intelligence, capability, and creativity. In one of his most moving speeches on May 5, 1962, Malcolm challenged African Americans to discard the lies of racial prejudice and accept themselves for who they were. "Who taught you to hate the texture of your hair?" he thundered. "Who taught you to hate the color of your skin? Who taught you to hate the shape of your nose and the shape of your lips? Who taught you to hate yourself from the top of your head to the soles of your feet? Who taught you to hate your own kind?" Malcolm would also later write, "One thing the white man never can give the black man is self-respect! The black man in America has to lift up his own sense of values."

By 1963, Malcolm X was considered to be one of the most popular speakers for college campuses. He had visited over 50 universities including Harvard and Yale. He often began panel discussions by announcing, "Gentlemen, I finished the eighth grade in Mason, Michigan. My high school was the black ghetto of Roxbury, Massachusetts. My college was in the streets of Harlem, and my master's was taken in prison."

Malcolm had personally established additional Nation of Islam temples in both Queens and Brooklyn of New

York City, as well as assisting to some degree in the founding of the more than one hundred other temples in existence. He was appointed the first national minister of the Nation of Islam.

But, he was hiding a secret.

For years, Malcolm had desperately tried not to believe the truth, deliberately ignoring the growing evidence. He could not face the fact that his confidence in the Nation of Islam and its leader, Elijah Muhammad, was completely undeserved. Malcolm himself claimed to have lived an utterly clean, moral life since his reform in prison. The same could not be said for Elijah, the man responsible for ordering the shunning of all Muslims convicted of sexual immorality, including Malcolm's own brother Reginald.

In the past, a numerous succession of Elijah's secretaries had become pregnant. Elijah allowed each of these women to be brought before a religious court, tried for adultery, humiliated, and banned from Muslim fellowship. Now two of them were issuing paternity suits against Elijah for their four children. "I had faith in the Nation," Malcolm mourned. Nonetheless, he began to hope that Elijah's good deeds would weigh more heavily in the public's estimation than his monstrous deception and betrayal.

In April of 1963, Malcolm visited Elijah at his current home in Phoenix, Arizona, where the man calmly admitted his sexual immorality. When Malcolm brokenheartedly offered him an excuse for his behavior by comparing him with popular Old Testament figures who had fallen into sin, Elijah was quick to accept the comparison. In fact, he claimed that his position as a prophet actually required a plunge into immorality.

In November of that year, Malcolm spoke shortly after the assassination of President John F. Kennedy, stating that the death of the president was "a case of the chickens coming home to roost." Aware of his deeply ingrained hatred for the American government, the public was indignant at this salt thrown on their still-bleeding wounds. Malcolm later tried to soften the remark by writing that he merely meant that "America's climate of hate had been responsible for the President's death" and that "some of the world's most important personages" were saying the same thing. On his visit to Elijah on the following day, however, Malcolm found that Elijah had suspended him from any activity within the Nation of Islam for the next 90 days on the pretext that Malcolm's remarks might put the Nation of Islam in a bad light in the public eye.

As rumors drifted, Malcolm realized that this was only Elijah Muhammad's first step in disassociating him with the Nation of Islam, the religion that Malcolm himself had been largely responsible for bringing into full existence. "My head felt like it was bleeding inside," he anguished.

Malcolm and his family went on vacation to visit and support Cassius Clay in Florida. The boxer was originally named after a staunch anti-slavery hero, but he would later rename himself Muhammad Ali—potentially not realizing that this name historically belonged to an

Egyptian slave trader known for kidnapping and exploiting Africans. Nevertheless, true to Nation of Islam traditions, Cassius Clay rejected his birth name, claiming that it was a "slave name."

In spite of the Nation of Islam's strict prohibition of sports, Malcolm energetically supported the boxer's famous fight against Sonny Liston on February 25, 1964, telling him that "It's the Cross and the Crescent fighting in a prize ring. It's a modern Crusades—a Christian and a Muslim facing each other" and asking him to celebrate what he considered a victory for Allah with ice cream at his motel room afterward.

Chapter Seven

Final Years and Assassination

"We're not Americans. We're Africans who happen to be in America. I'm not interested in being an American."

—Malcolm X

The Nation of Islam ordered the murder of Malcolm X in 1964. The member who was instructed to create a car bomb had been a former friend of Malcolm's, and he decided to reveal the truth to Malcolm instead of taking his life.

Now aware that he could be assassinated at any time, Malcolm decided to leave the Nation of Islam and build an organization of his own. Before the first meeting was held, everyone from disillusioned NOI members to white people who were tired of the snail's pace of the civil rights movement flooded Malcolm with support. Malcolm would become the head of Muslim Mosque, Inc., based in New York City. He would live with "constant awareness that any number of my former brothers felt they would make heroes of themselves in the Nation of Islam if they killed me. I knew how Elijah Muhammad's followers thought; I had taught so many of them to think." The violent fanatics that Malcolm had trained were now on his own trail.

But there was one place Malcolm felt he could go for safety and support; he would make his religious pilgrimage to Mecca. Once off his hated American soil and relaxed and trusting among fellow Muslims, Malcolm became amazed at the way that disparate nations and ethnicities, light-skinned and dark-skinned, could mingle happily with one another. "It was like pages out of the *National Geographic* magazine," he observed.

Nonetheless, there was trouble with Malcolm's passport. Since no non-Muslim was permitted to enter Mecca, the religious leaders wanted to be sure that Malcolm's conversion was authentic. As he waited and watched the people about him, Malcolm realized that the rituals he had been taught in the Nation of Islam were not quite the same as the rituals practiced by other Muslims around the world. Malcolm felt humiliated that he, as the former national minister of the Nation of Islam, actually knew so little about the Muslim religion.

Eventually Malcolm was treated to the lavish hospitality of a wealthy white Muslim who promised to make sure that Malcolm would be able to complete his pilgrimage. Freed from his racial prejudices through his feelings of kinship with other Muslims, Malcolm felt very differently toward this white man than he had felt toward the white people of America. "That morning was the start of a radical alteration in my whole outlook about 'white' men," Malcolm would later remember.

Malcolm was able to complete the traditional pilgrimage through the Mosque of Mecca, and after observing the brotherhood of Muslim people of all races, he emerged convinced that racism—which he had spent his entire life in promoting through his furious hatred of all white people—was a great evil.

After touring the Holy Land, Malcolm visited Beirut, Cairo, Alexandria, Nigeria, Ghana, and Algiers, speaking to everyone he met about white oppression of black people in America. "I knew that any American white man with a genuine brotherhood for a black man was hard to find, no matter how much he grinned," Malcolm wrote.

Although Malcolm's perspectives and message had changed when he returned to America, the problems had not—and neither had the public's memory of the embittered, hate-filled speeches Malcolm had poured into their ears for the past 12 years. It was hard for white society to trust the intentions of this man who had long labeled them as "devils" when he now spoke of benefitting humanity as a whole.

When Malcolm spoke reasonably about African American's natural human right to defend themselves if necessary, it was difficult for his listeners to forget the unbridled violence that he had advocated before his trip to Mecca. In the past, Malcolm had often refused to acknowledge as genuine the goodwill which had been offered to him by white individuals—and now the tables were turned. Malcolm was impatient with the public's reluctance to accept his sudden change. Neither did he give credit to the fact that his former teachings had given birth to a violent, hate-filled creed, especially among black youth, that was now beyond his own power to control.

Soon Malcolm left home to travel further in the Middle East and Africa, becoming more convinced than ever that the United States of America was the source of most racism in the world and that so-called liberal Democrats actually cared no more for African Americans than conservative Republicans, but simply used the race issue to further their own political power-grasping.

Upon his return to America, Malcolm worked on his newly formed Black Nationalist organization, the Organization of Afro-American Unity (OAAU), that would first teach African Americans to respect themselves before helping them to defeat racism. His first task, however, was to change his public image and convince America that he had a new message to bring to them.

Although he did not permit white people to join his organization, rightfully feeling that African Americans needed to recognize their capacity to accomplish things by themselves, Malcolm now responded kindly to white people who sought to support his cause, a vast change from his former attitudes. "In our mutual sincerity we might be able to show a road to the salvation of America's very soul," he reflected. "It can only be salvaged if human rights and dignity, in full, are extended to black men." No longer did Malcolm ridicule and repudiate civil rights activists such as Martin Luther King, Jr. for their patience, nonviolence, and willingness to work alongside white leaders. Slowly, Malcolm's image was changing.

Although history would never be able to fully forget Malcolm X's flaming speeches of hatred and rage, people would also be able to remember his maturing conviction of the equality of all races and admit with him that "you're not supposed to be so blind with patriotism that you can't face reality. Wrong is wrong, no matter who says it."

Malcolm himself lived with the expectation of being assassinated at any moment, aware that he still had powerful enemies in the Nation of Islam. The religious organization already had filed a lawsuit against him to evacuate him from the home in Queens with which he had been provided when he married Betty. Malcolm had always trusted the Nation of Islam to provide for his family if they were in need. Now he faced financial difficulties and the realization that his pregnant wife and four small daughters would certainly receive no support from the Nation of Islam if he should be killed.

The organizational burdens of the OAAU lay heavy on his shoulders as well. Somehow, Malcolm seemed less successful at pulling people together now that he had become more tolerant in his ideas than he had been in the past when he was rightfully labeled as a dangerous firebrand. Neither the more militant activists nor the moderates found a balanced Malcolm to be to their taste.

What did not change was that Malcolm was just as frenetically active as before, traveling, speaking, and writing for the cause of the African American, even as death threats began to pour in and legitimate worry about his family's safety increased. After all, Malcolm had not only abandoned the Nation of Islam—whose violent character the man who had done the most to form it knew only too well—but he had completely forsaken its principles of racial segregation, stating that "I recognize every human being as a human being. When you are dealing with humanity as a family there's no question of integration or intermarriage. It's just one human being marrying another human being."

On January 28, 1965, Malcolm was surrounded by members of the Nation of Islam while in a hotel in Los Angeles. The men threateningly followed him in cars as he was driven to the airport. For days, while providing testimony before the Attorney General in Chicago, Illinois, about the activities of the Nation of Islam, Malcolm had to be constantly protected by the police against this machine of hatred that he himself had formed.

Malcolm continued with his speaking itinerary, although his nerves were strained and he felt certain that the end of his life was near. He made a visit to France and London, returning on February 13 to endure being attacked with homemade bombs during the night while sleeping at home with his family. Everyone managed to escape the burning house in time, but their home was destroyed. Malcolm's wife and children had to seek shelter with friends while Malcolm himself left for another speaking engagement in Detroit, followed, of course, by still more interviews and lectures.

Malcolm fully expected his coming assassination and felt that it would be a martyrdom for the cause of human brotherhood. "[Brotherhood] is the only thing that can save this country," he stated to a reporter. "I've learned it the hard way—but I've learned it. I did many things as a Muslim that I'm sorry for now."

On February 21, 1965, Malcolm X was scheduled to give an address at the Audubon Ballroom in New York City. During his speech, there was a sudden disturbance near the front of the seated crowd. As everyone turned to see what was going on, men suddenly leaped from the front row, drew weapons, and began repeatedly firing on the speaker. Malcolm's tall body tumbled backward over the chairs behind him as blood gushed from wounds in his chest, head, hands, and legs. In the audience, his wife threw her own body, pregnant with twins, over her four screaming little daughters.

People crouched on the floors for safety. Others rushed the stage to give assistance to the dying man. Police clutched at potential suspects as members of the distraught crowd fled in every direction. Malcolm was already dead when the ambulance arrived with him at the hospital.

It was difficult to find a church not too frightened to host a funeral for Malcolm X. When one was located, multiple bomb threats were telephoned to the church. The nation held its breath in fear of rioting in Harlem. A Nation of Islam temple was burned to the ground, along with several of the buildings beside it. Strikes were threatened toward any stores that would remain open during the funeral. Worldwide, newspapers reported their opinions of the tragedy. The extent of the confusion was hard to describe.

From February 23 through 26, crowds of many thousands of mourners filed past the casket of Malcolm X before he would be prepared for a Muslim funeral and burial on February 27, 1965.

But not all of Malcolm's' friends believed that his murder had been accomplished by the Nation of Islam. Many complained that police protection of the event in the Audubon Ballroom had been woefully inadequate. Malcolm himself had begun dropping hints in the days immediately before his death that he was uncertain that the Nation of Islam was actually capable of orchestrating the threats and persecution that he had received during those final days.

Eventually one Nation of Islam member, however, who was captured by police on the scene, would fully admit to taking part in the murder. Two others were also implicated, though they insisted on their innocence. All three men were sentenced to life in prison. With no concrete evidence against him, Elijah Muhammad escaped punishment.

Conclusion

The evolving message of Malcolm X, stained though it was by his early expressions of race hatred, left one clear conviction behind—every African American is a human being, a person with value and rights equal to that of any other person on earth.

Regretful at some of the words he had spoken but never ashamed of his righteous anger against racial injustice, Malcolm confided, "Sometimes, I have dared to dream to myself that one day history may even say that my voice—which disturbed the white man's smugness, and his arrogance, and his complacency—that my voice helped to save America from a grave, possibly even a fatal catastrophe."

Printed in Great Britain
by Amazon